Cheap AND *Easy!*

MAYTAG DRYER REPAIR

2000 EDITION

Written ESPECIALLY for Trade Schools,
Do-It-Yourselfers, and other "green" technicians!

By Douglas Emley

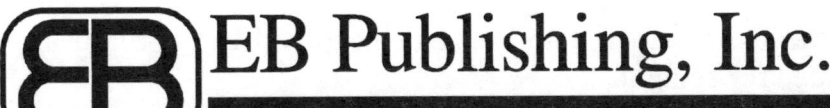

EB Publishing, Inc.

Carson City, Nevada ● Phone / Fax toll free 888-974-1224 ● website: http://www.appliancerepair.net

The Author, the publisher and all interested parties have used all possible care to assure that the information contained in this book is as complete and as accurate as possible. However, neither the publisher nor the author nor any interested party assumes any liability for omissions, errors, or defects in the materials, instructions or diagrams contained in this publication, and therefore are not liable for any damages including (but not limited to) personal injury, property damage or legal disputes that may result from the use of this book.

All major appliances are complex electro-mechanical devices. Personal injury or property damage may occur before, during, or after any attempt to repair an appliance. This publication is intended for individuals posessing an adequate background of technical experience. The above named parties are not responsible for an individual's judgement of his or her own technical abilities and experience, and therefore are not liable for any damages including (but not limited to) personal injury, property damage or legal disputes that may result from such judgements.

The advice and opinions offered by this publication are of a subjective nature ONLY and they are NOT to be construed as legal advice. The above named parties are not responsible for the interpretation or implementation of subjective advice and opinions, and therefore are not responsible for any damages including (but not limited to) personal injury, property damage, or legal disputes that may result from such interpretation or implementation.

The use of this publication acknowledges the understanding and acceptance of the above terms and conditions.

Maytag®, Norge®, Admiral® and Magic Chef® are registered trademarks of the Maytag Corporation, Newton, Iowa, USA.

Special Thanks to technical consultant Dick Miller, whose forty years of experience as a field appliance service technician are reflected in the technical information and procedures described in this publication.

Published by EB Publishing, Inc., 251 Jeanell Drive Suite 3, Carson City, NV 89703

This service manual was excerpted from EB Publishing's Cheap and Easy! Clothes Dryer Repair Manual and edited for content.

Printed in the United States of America

HOW TO USE THIS BOOK

STEP 1: READ THE DISCLAIMERS ON THE PREVIOUS PAGE. This book is intended for use by people who have a bit of mechanical experience or aptitude, and just need a little coaching when it comes to appliances. If you don't fit that category, don't use this book! We're all bloomin' lawyers these days, y'know? If you break something or hurt yourself, no one is responsible but **YOU**; not the author, the publisher, the guy or the store who sold you this book, or anyone else. Only **YOU** are responsible, and just by using this book, you're agreeing to that and more. If you don't understand the disclaimers, get a lawyer to translate them **before** you start working.

Read the safety and repair precautions in section 1-5. These should help you avoid making too many *really* bad mistakes.

STEP 2: READ CHAPTERS 1 & 2: Everything else in this book flows from chapters 1 and 2. If you don't read them, you won't be able to properly diagnose your dryer.

Know what kind of dryer you have and basically how it works. When you go to the appliance parts dealer, have the nameplate information at hand. Have the proper tools at hand, and know how to use them.

STEP 3: READ THE CHAPTER ABOUT YOUR SPECIFIC MODEL.

STEP 4: FIX THE BLOOMIN' THING! If you can, of course. If you're just too confused, or if the book recommends calling a technician for a complex operation, call one.

WHAT THIS BOOK WILL DO FOR YOU
(and what it won't!)

This book **will** tell you how to fix the most common problems with the most common brands of domestic (household) dryers. (This represents 95+ percent of all repairs that the average handyman or service tech will run into.)

This book **will not** tell you how to fix your industrial or commercial or any very large dryer. The support and control systems for such units are usually very similar in function to those of smaller units, but vastly different in design, service and repair.

We **will** show you the easiest and/or fastest method of diagnosing and repairing your dryer.

We **will not necessarily** show you the absolute cheapest way of doing something. Sometimes, when the cost of a part is just a few dollars, we advocate replacing the part rather than rebuilding it. We also sometimes advocate replacement of an inexpensive part, whether it's good or bad, as a simplified method of diagnosis or as a preventive measure.

We **will** use only the simplest of tools; tools that a well-equipped home mechanic is likely to have and to know how to use, including a VOM.

We **will not** advocate your buying several hundred dollars' worth of exotic equipment or special tools, or getting advanced technical training to make a one-time repair. It will usually cost you less to have a professional perform this type of repair. Such repairs represent only a very small percentage of all needed repairs.

We **do not** discuss electrical or mechanical theories. There are already many very well-written textbooks on these subjects and most of them are not likely to be pertinent to the job at hand; fixing your dryer!

We **do** discuss rudimentary mechanical systems and simple electrical circuits.

We expect you to be able to look at a part and remove it if the mounting bolts and/or connections are obvious. If the mounting mechanism is complicated or hidden, or there are tricks to removing or installing something, we'll tell you about it.

You are expected to know what certain electrical and mechanical devices are, what they do in general, and how they work. For example, switches, relays, heater elements, motors, solenoids, cams, pullies, idlers, belts, radial and thrust (axial) bearings, flexible motor couplings, splines, gas valves, air seals, and centrifugal blowers and axial-flow fans. If you do not know what these things do, learn them BEFORE you start working on your dryer.

You should know how to cut, strip, and splice wire with crimp-on connectors, wire nuts and electrical tape. You should know how to measure voltage and how to test for continuity with a VOM (Volt-Ohm Meter). If you have an ammeter, you should know how and where to measure the current in amps. If you don't know how to use these meters, there's a brief course on how to use them (for *our* purposes *only*) in Chapter 1. See section 1-4 before you buy either or both of these meters.

A given procedure was only included in this manual if it passed the following criteria:

1) The job is something that the average couch potato can complete in one afternoon, with no prior knowledge of the machine, with tools a normal home handyman is likely to have.

2) The parts and/or special tools required to complete the job are easily found and not too expensive.

3) The problem is a common one; occuring more frequently than just one out of a hundred machines.

Certain more expensive repairs may be included in this manual only if they pass the following criteria:

1) The cost of the repair is far less than replacing the machine or calling a professional service technician, and

2) The repair is likely to yield a machine that will operate satisfactorily for several more years, or at least long enough to justify the cost.

In certain parts of the book, the author may express an opinion as to whether the current value of a particular machine warrants making the repair or "scrapping" the machine. Such opinions are to be construed as opinions ONLY and they are NOT to be construed as legal advice. The decision as to whether to take a particular machine out of service depends on a number of factors that the author cannot possibly know and has no control over; therefore, the responsibility for such a decision rests solely with the person making the decision.

I'm sure that a physicist reading this book could have a lot of fun tearing it apart because of my deliberate avoidance and misuse of technical terms. However, this manual is written to simplify the material and inform the novice, not to appease the scientist.

*NOTE: The diagnosis and repair procedures in this manual do not necessarily apply to brand-new units, newly-installed units or recently relocated units. Although they **may** posess the problems described in this manual, dryers that have recently been installed or moved are subject to special considerations not taken into account in this manual for the sake of simplicity. Such special considerations include installation parameters, installation location, the possibility of manufacturing or construction defects, damage in transit, and others.*

This manual was designed to assist the novice technician in the repair of home (domestic) dryers that have been operating successfully for an extended period of months or years and have only recently stopped operating properly, with no major change in installation parameters or location.

Table Of Contents

Chapter 1

DRYER IDENTIFICATION
TOOLS & SAFETY
TIPS & TRICKS

1-1. BRAND IDENTIFICATION

This service manual covers Maytag brand dryers only. Not long ago, Maycor bought out the Norge / Magic Chef / Admiral brands; however, these brands are are built to a different design and are not covered in this manual.

In the mid 1980's, Maytag began selling a completely redesigned dryer. Prior to that, they sold a design called a "halo of heat" model. These older machines were well-built and there are still a vast number of them in service.

The easiest way to tell them apart is that in the "halo" models, the lint screen is inside the center rear of the drum, whereas the late model Maytag machines have the lint screen in the front of the cabinet, at the bottom of the door opening.

1-2 BEFORE YOU START

Find yourself a good appliance parts dealer. You can find them in the yellow pages under the following headings:

● APPLIANCES, HOUSEHOLD, MAJOR
● APPLIANCES, PARTS AND SUPPLIES
● REFRIGERATORS, DOMESTIC
● APPLIANCES, HOUSEHOLD, REPAIR
   AND SERVICE

Call a few of them and ask if they are a repair service, or if they sell parts, or both. Ask them if they offer free advice with the parts they sell. (Occasionally, stores that offer both parts and service will not want to give you advice.) Often the parts counter men are ex-technicians who got tired of the pressures of in-home service. They can be your best friends. However, you don't want to badger them with TOO many questions, so know your basics before you start asking questions.

Some parts houses may offer service, too. Be careful! There may be a conflict of interest. They may try to talk you out of even trying to fix your own dryer. They'll tell you it's too complicated, then in the same breath "guide" you to their service department. Who are you gonna believe, me or them? Not all service and parts places are this way, however. If they genuinely try to help you fix it yourself, and you find that you're unable to, they may be the best place to look for service.

When you go into the store, have ready the make, model and serial number from the nameplate of the dryer.

NAMEPLATE INFORMATION

The metal nameplate is usually found inside the door.

If it's wiped out or you can't find it, check the original papers that came with your dryer when it was new. They should contain the model number somewhere.

In any case, and especially if you have absolutely NO information about your dryer anywhere, make sure you bring your old part to the parts store with you. Sometimes they can match it up by looks or by part number.

1-3 TOOLS (Figure B-2)

The tools that you may need (depending on the diagnosis) are listed below.

Some are optional. The reason for the option is explained.

For certain repairs, you will need a special tool. These are inexpensively available from your appliance parts dealer. They are listed in this book as needed.

SCREWDRIVERS: Both flat and phillips head; two or three sizes of each. It's best to have at least a stubby, 4- and 6-inch sizes.

NUTDRIVERS: You will need at least 1/4" and 5/16" sizes. 4- or 6-inch ones should suffice, but it's better to have a stubby, too. A certain procedure when working on gas valves (Chapter 2, replacing the split coil assembly) requires a 7/32" nutdriver in most cases.

Figure B-2: Tools

Screwdrivers:
Flat
Phillips
Nutdrivers: 1/4" and 5/16"
Alligator Jumpers
Pliers
Diagonals
Electrician's
Volt-Ohmmeter

ELECTRICAL PLIERS or STRIPPERS and DIAGONAL CUTTING PLIERS: For cutting and stripping small electrical wire.

ALLIGATOR JUMPERS *(sometimes called a "CHEATER" or "CHEATER WIRE":)* Small guage (14-16 guage or so) and about 12-18 inches long, for testing electrical circuits. Available at your local electronics store. Cost: a few bucks for 4 or 5 of them.

BUTT CONNECTORS, CRIMPERS, WIRE NUTS and ELECTRICAL TAPE: For splicing small wire.

VOM (VOLT-OHM METER) For testing electrical circuits. If you do not have one, get one. An inexpensive one will suffice, as long as it has both "AC Voltage" and "Resistance" (i.e. Rx1, Rx10)

settings on the dial. It will do for our purposes.

OPTIONAL TOOLS (Figure B-3)

SNAP-AROUND AMMETER: For determining if electrical components are energized. Quite useful; but a bit expensive, and there are alternate methods. If you have one, use it; otherwise, don't bother getting one.

EXTENDABLE INSPECTION MIRROR: For seeing difficult places beneath the dryer and behind panels.

CORDLESS POWER SCREWDRIVER OR DRILL/DRIVER WITH MAGNETIC SCREWDRIVER AND NUTDRIVER TIPS: For pulling off panels held in place by many screws. It can save you lots of time and hassle.

Figure B-3: Optional Tools

Extendible Inspection Mirror

Clip-Around Ammeter

Cordless Power Drill-Driver and Tips

Nut Driver

Flat Screwdriver

Phillips Screwdriver

1-4. HOW TO USE A VOM AND AMMETER

Many home handymen are very intimidated by electricity. It's true that diagnosing and repairing electrical circuits requires a *bit* more care than most operations, due to the danger of getting shocked. But there is no mystery or voodoo about the things we'll be doing. Remember the rule in section 1-5(1); while you are working on a circuit, energize the circuit only long enough to perform whatever test you're performing, then take the power back off it to perform the repair. You need not be concerned with any theory, like what an ohm is, or what a volt is. You will only need to be able to set the VOM onto the right scale, touch the test leads to the right place and read the meter.

In using the VOM (Volt-Ohm Meter) for our purposes, the two test leads are always plugged into the "+" and "-" holes on the VOM. (Some VOMs have more than two holes.)

1-4(a). TESTING VOLTAGE (Figure B-4)

Set the dial of the VOM on the lowest VAC scale (A.C. Voltage) over 120 volts. For example, if there's a 50 setting and a 250 setting on the VAC dial, use the 250 scale, because 250 is the lowest setting over 120 volts.

Touch the two test leads to the two metal contacts of a live power source, like a wall outlet or the terminals of the motor that you're testing for voltage. (*Do not* **jam** *the test leads into a wall outlet!*) If you are getting power through the VOM, the meter will jump up and steady on a reading. You *may* have to convert the scale in your head. For example, if you're using the 250 volt dial setting and the meter has a "25" scale, simply divide by 10; 120 volts would be "12" on the meter.

Figure B-4: Testing Voltage

Set VOM on the proper A.C. Voltage scale

Correct reading is 110 to 125 Volts

Do not jam or force test leads into wall outlet

Standard Wall Outlet

Component being tested for voltage (in this case, a solenoid)

Solenoid Leads

Touch Test leads to Metal Contacts (i.e. terminals or bare wire ends)

A word of caution: 220 Volts can be dangerous stuff!!! When testing 220 volt circuits (usually in electric dryers) make sure you always follow the precautions in rule 1 of section 1-5!

1-4(b). TESTING FOR CONTINUITY (Figure B-5)

Don't let the word "continuity" scare you. It's derived from the word "continuous." In an electrical circuit, electricity has to flow *from* a power source back *to* that power source. If there is any break in the circuit, it is not continuous, and it has no continuity. "Good" continuity means that there is no break in the circuit.

For example, if you were testing a solenoid to see if it was burned out, you would try putting a small amount of power through the solenoid. If it was burned out, there would be a break in the circuit, the electricity wouldn't flow, and your meter would show no continuity.

That is what the resistance part of your VOM does; it provides a small electrical current (using batteries within the VOM) and measures how fast the current is flowing. For our purposes, it doesn't matter how *fast* the current is flowing; only that there *is* current flow.

To use your VOM to test continuity, set the dial on (resistance) R x 1, or whatever the lowest setting is. Touch the metal parts of the test leads together and read the meter. It should peg the meter all the way on the right side of the scale, towards "0" on the meter's "resistance" scale. If the meter does not read zero resistance, adjust the thumbwheel on the front of the VOM until it *does* read zero. If you cannot get the meter to read zero, the battery in the VOM is low; replace it.

If you are testing, say, a solenoid, first make sure that the solenoid leads are not connected to anything, especially a power source. If the solenoid's leads are still connected to something, you may get a reading through that something. If there is still live power on the item

Figure B-5: Testing Continuity

No need to remove the component from the dryer. Just disconnect power and isolate the component electrically. First, set the meter to the lowest resistance scale; (usually R X 1.)

Then touch the test leads together and zero the meter using the thumbwheel.

Then touch test leads to metal or bare wire ends.

Good Continuity: meter needle moves towards right side of scale.

Bad Continuity: meter needle stays towards left side of scale.

you're testing for continuity, you will burn out your VOM instantly and possibly shock yourself.

Touch the two test leads to the two bare wire ends or terminals of the solenoid. You can touch the ends of the wires and test leads with your hands if necessary to get better contact. The voltage that the VOM batteries put out is very low, and you will not be shocked. If there is NO continuity, the meter won't move. If there is GOOD continuity, the meter will move toward the right side of the scale and steady on a reading. This is the resistance reading and it doesn't concern us; we only care that we show good continuity. If the meter moves only very little and stays towards the left side of the scale, that's BAD continuity; the solenoid is no good.

If you are testing a switch, you will show little or no resistance (good continuity) when the switch is closed, and NO continuity when the switch is open. If you do not, the switch is bad.

1-4(c). AMMETERS

Ammeters are a little bit more complex to explain without going into a lot of electrical theory. If you own an ammeter, you probably already know how to use it.

If you don't, don't get one. Ammeters are expensive. And for *our* purposes, there are other ways to determine what an ammeter tests for. If you don't own one, skip this section.

For our purposes, ammeters are simply a way of testing for continuity without having to cut into the system or to disconnect power from whatever it is we're testing.

Ammeters measure the current in amps flowing through a wire. The greater the current that's flowing *through* a wire, the greater the density of the magnetic field, or *flux*, it produces *around* the wire. The ammeter simply measures the density of this flux, and thus the amount of current, flowing

Figure B-6: Testing Amperage

No need to remove the component from the dryer

Connected to a power source.

Clip ammeter around one lead only.

No continuity: component not operating. Break somewhere in circuit. Drawing zero amps.

Set ammeter to an appropriate scale, say 0-10 or 0-20 amps

Connected to a power source.

Good continuity: Component operating. Drawing significant amps.

through the wire. To determine continuity, for our purposes, we can simply isolate the component that we're testing (so we do not accidentally measure the current going through any other components) and see if there's *any* current flow.

To use your ammeter, first make sure that it's on an appropriate scale (0 to 10 or 20 amps will do). Isolate a wire leading directly to the component you're testing. Put the ammeter loop around that wire and read the meter. (Figure B-6)

1-5. BASIC REPAIR AND SAFETY PRECAUTIONS

1) Always de-energize (pull the plug or trip the breaker on) any dryer that you're disassembling. If you need to re-energize the dryer to perform a test, make sure any bare wires or terminals are taped or insulated. Energize the unit only long enough to perform whatever test you're performing, then disconnect the power again.

I want to impress upon you something really important. In electric dryers, you're usually dealing with 220 volt circuits. DO NOT TAKE THIS LIGHTLY. I've been hit with 110 volts now and then. Anyone who works with electrical equipment has at one time or another. It's unpleasant, but unless exposure is more than a second or so, the only harm it usually does is to tick you off pretty good. However, *220 VOLTS CAN KNOCK YOU OFF YOUR FEET. IT CAN DO YOUR BODY SOME SERIOUS DAMAGE, VERY QUICKLY. DO NOT TEST LIVE 220 VOLT CIRCUITS.*

If you have a heart condition, epilepsy, or other potentially serious health conditions, well...hey, it's just my opinion, but you shouldn't be testing 220 volt circuits *at all*. It's not worth dying for.

2) If this manual advocates replacing a part, REPLACE IT!! You might find, say, a solenoid that has jammed for no apparent reason. Sometimes you can clean it out and lubricate it, and get it going again. The key words here are *apparent reason*. There is a reason that it stopped. You can bet on it. And if you get it going and re-install it, you are running a very high risk that it will stop again. If *that* happens, you will have to start repairing your dryer *all* over again. It may only act up when it is hot, or it may be bent slightly...there are a hundred different "what if's." Very few of the parts mentioned in this book will cost you over ten or twenty dollars. Replace the part.

3) If you must lay the dryer over on its side, front or back, first make sure that you are not going to break anything off, such as a gas valve. Lay an old blanket on the floor to protect the floor and the finish of the dryer.

4) Always replace the green (ground) leads when you remove an electrical component. They're there for a reason. And NEVER EVER remove the third (ground) prong in the main power plug!

5) When opening the dryer cabinet or console, remember that the sheet metal parts are have very sharp edges. Wear gloves, and be careful not to cut your hands!

6) When testing for your power supply from a wall outlet, plug in a small appliance such as a shaver or blow dryer. If you're not getting full power out of the outlet, you'll know it right away.

7) If you have diagnosed a certain part to be bad, but you cannot figure out how to remove it, sometimes it helps to get the new part and examine it for mounting holes or other clues as to how it may be mounted.

Chapter 2

GENERAL OPERATION AND COMPONENT DIAGNOSIS

2-1 DRYER BASICS & COMPONENTS

The main idea of a dryer is to circulate warm air through wet clothes to evaporate moisture from them. This sounds really simple, but there are many implications. This means that all dryers have to have a blower to move air and a heat source to warm the air, and that airflow is very important. It also means that all dryers must have a way to toss the clothes around a bit, because air won't circulate through them if they're just laying there in a big wet lump. This is done by "tumbling" them in a big round drum.

2-1(a) DRIVE TRAIN (Figure G-1)

All dryers have a drive motor which turns the drum through a belt. In most dryers, the motor also turns a blower fan connected directly to the motor shaft; in early model machines (Chapter 4) the fan is belted off the drive motor, too.

Figure G-1: Generic Drive Train

2-1(b) HEAT SOURCE AND TEMPERATURE CONTROL

Warm air evaporates moisture much faster than cold air, so all dryers also have a heat source. The heat source in household machines is either gas or electric. Electric heating elements come in many different configurations; see chapter 3 or 4 about your machine for details. Gas burners are remarkably similar in all the different models. Ignitor systems and holding coils on the gas safety valves have varied slightly over the years, but you can find the diagnosis and repair procedures for all gas burners covered by this manual in section 2-3.

A temperature control system keeps the air at the optimum temperature for drying and prevents scorching of your clothes. This system uses several thermostats; some adjustable and others a fixed temperature. Testing the temperature control system is discussed in section 2-4(c). Finding the thermostats is discussed in the chapters 3 & 4 pertaining to your model.

There is also a safety system that prevents the heating system from starting at all unless the blower is turning. This prevents overheating of the system or natural gas buildup in the dryer cabinet. A contact in the centrifugal motor starting switch assembly only allows the heating system to heat if the motor is running.

2-1(c) AIRFLOW, LINT FILTER AND EXHAUST SYSTEM

Airflow is important in removing the moisture from the dryer drum; thus the blower, vents and exhaust ducting must be kept as clean (translation: free of lint)

as possible. This also prevents overheating of electric heating elements and accidental lint fires, and insures enough airflow to keep the gas burner operating properly.

Also, drum seals can wear out and leak, which can disrupt proper airflow.

The lint screen traps most lint, but some does get through or leak out around the drum seals. Over a period of years enough can build up enough to allow some of the above symptoms to occur. The airflow system is discussed in section 2-5, except for drum seals, which are discussed in the chapters 3 and 4.

The blower is the last component in the airflow system. (See Figure G-1) From the blower, the air goes directly out the dryer exhaust. Thus, the other components are *not* under *pressure*. Air is being *sucked* through them, so they are under a *vacuum*.

2-1(d) TIMERS AND OTHER CONTROLS

Some dryer timers are simply devices that run the motor for a set number of minutes; others integrate temperature control and even moisture (humidity) controls. Yet others are solid-state, electronic units. If you have a separate timer and temperature control, consider yourself lucky; the combined units are considerably more difficult to diagnose and generally more expensive to replace. Diagnosis is discussed in Chapter 2-4(b).

2-2 SYMPTOMS

Dryers are relatively simple machines; they just don't have many components. So most repairs stem from just a few common complaints:

1) NOISY OPERATION

See chapter 3 or 4 about your model.

2) NOT DRYING WELL, DRYING MORE SLOWLY THAN USUAL, OR NO HEAT AT ALL

Usually this is caused by poor airflow. Feel the dryer vent exhaust (usually outside the house.) If there isn't a strong blast of air coming out, check the lint screen and open up any dryer vent you can get to to check for clogging. Also check any flexible dryer vent for pinching. Remove the dryer vent from the back of the machine and see if the air blast feels stronger. If so, you probably have clogged vent ducting.

If the drum is not turning, there may be no noise or other external symptoms. The clothes will simply be laying there in a big wet lump and they won't dry. The dryer probably won't *sound* normal either. To diagnose, start the machine empty, open the door and look inside quickly, or depress the door switch to see if the drum is turning. If not, the belt or belt tensioner may be broken. To repair, see the chapter about your brand.

You may see similar symptoms if the motor has gone bad, except that you probably will not hear the motor turning. If the motor is locked, you may hear it buzzing. See section 2-4(d) about motors.

There may also be a problem with some other component the air heating system within the dryer. See section 2-4(c) about thermostats and temperature control systems, section 2-3(a) about gas burners, or section 2-4(f) and the chapter about your model for information about electric heating elements.

2-3 GAS BURNERS (Figure G-2)

Gas burners can generally be divided into two broad categories; pilot and pilotless ignition. Pilot ignition models have not been manufactured in a number of years, and thus tend to be older units, but there are still a significant number of

Figure G-2: Gas Burners

Flame Spreader

Air Mixing Ports

Gas Valve Solenoids (Split Coil Assembly)

Burner Chamber

Venturi

Flame Switch

Ignitor

Gas Valve

Note: Burner assembly shown with wiring removed for clarity

them in operation. All of the older "Halo of Heat" models had pilot ignition.

The main components of the system (see Figure G-2) are the gas valve, venturi and burner chamber, and gas safety solenoids (in all models,) the flame sensor and the ignitor (in pilotless models,) or the pilot orifice and sensor (in pilot models.)

IGNITORS

See figure G-3 for pictures of the different types of ignitors.

Most ignitors just glow until the mechanism opens the gas valve. The "warp switch" ignitor sparks to ignite the gas (see "NORMAL BURNER OPERATION" below.) If you have a "glo-sil" ignitor, (it looks like a tiny coil) and it is burnt out, you are probably out of luck. They are difficult and expensive to get parts for, and considering the age of these dryers, you will probably end up getting a new dryer.

NORMAL BURNER OPERATION

A normally operating gas burner system will have a clean, mostly blue flame (perhaps occasionally streaked with just a little tinge of orange) that cycles on and off every couple of minutes.

When the flame is off and starts to cycle on, you will hear a loud click. In a pilot system, the gas valve will open and the flame will kick on at this time. In a pilotless system, the ignitor will heat up and glow brightly for about 7-15 seconds. The flame sensor senses the heat from the ignitor. If it is glowing, you will hear another click, the gas valve will open and the flame will kick on. This is a safety feature; if you don't have ignition, you certainly don't want to open the gas valve and dump gas into the dryer cabinet.

Models with a spark ignitor, or "warp switch" ignitor act slightly differently. Instead of the ignitor glowing, you will hear a metallic rattling sound and see what looks almost like a welder's arc flashing. The flame starts immediately and after about 15-20 seconds, the metallic rattling will stop but the flame will stay on.

When the air in the dryer drum reaches the chosen temperature (as sensed by the thermostats) the gas valve will close and the flame will shut off.

Figure G-3: Ignitors

Glo-Bar (Round) Ignitor

Glo-Bar (Flat) Ignitor

Typical Spark Ignitor (Warp Switch System)

Sparking Contacts

2-3(a) GAS BURNER SYMPTOMS AND REPAIR

IGNITOR DOESN'T GLOW (PILOTLESS SYSTEMS ONLY)

Nine times out of ten, if the ignitor is not glowing, it is burnt out. Unplug the dryer and remove the burner assembly as shown in figure G-4. Usually you will see a white or yellowish burned area and a break in the ignitor. If so, replace the ignitor. If you can't see an obvious break, test the ignitor for continuity as described in section 2-4(e).

If the ignitor is not defective, you need to isolate whether the problem is in the control (thermostat) area, or at the burner itself. The general idea is that if you have 110 volts getting to the burner assembly, then the thermostats are OK,

and something in the burner assembly is bad. If you don't have 110 volts at the burner, then a thermostat or some other control is bad.

Perform the following test:

1) Unplug the dryer and open the burner inspection cover as described in the chapter about your model.

2) Unplug the main wiring harness leading to the burner assembly. (Figure G-4)

3) Using your alligator jumpers, connect a VOM to the *dryer* side of the harness plug. (as opposed to the side of the harness plug that's connected to the *burner*.)

4) Make sure no wires will get caught up in the turning drum. Set your dryer timer to the "on" position, high heat, and plug in the dryer. If your VOM reads 110 volts, something in the burner assembly is bad. If the burner *isn't* getting voltage,

Figure G-4: Removing the Burner Assembly

Step ① UNPLUG YOUR DRYER!

Step ② Shut off manual gas valve, and disconnect gas pipe at the gas solenoid valve

Step ③ Disconnect wiring harness at plug

Dryer side of plug

Burner side of plug

Test here for power

Step ④ Remove wires from the flame sensor

Step ⑤ Remove the mounting screws

the problem is in one of the components of the heating control system: a thermostat, timer or temperature control switch, or motor centrifugal switch.

If you trace it to the burner assembly, and you've already eliminated the ignitor as the problem, either the flame sensor or the gas valve solenoid coil(s) are bad. Unplug the dryer, disconnect the flame sensor and test it for continuity. If you have no continuity, the flame sensor is bad. If you have continuity, the coils are bad. Bring the burner assembly to your parts dealer to make sure you get the right coil assembly, and don't forget to bring the model number of the machine.

SPARKER DOESN'T SPARK, OR FLAME DOESN'T START (WARP SWITCH SYSTEM ONLY)

In the older models mentioned previously, if you do not hear the metallic rattling sound, the ignitor may be out of adjustment. It can be a difficult and com-plex adjustment to make. Take the burner assembly to your parts dealer and they should be able to help you adjust it or guide you to someone who can.

IGNITOR GLOWS, BUT FLAME DOES NOT START (GAS VALVE DOES NOT OPEN) (PILOTLESS SYSTEMS ONLY)

Either the flame sensor is not working properly or the safety solenoid coils are not opening the gas valve. If the ignitor doesn't stop glowing, the flame sensor is bad. If the ignitor cycles on and off, the gas solenoid coil(s) are bad.

FLAME STARTS (GAS VALVE OPENS) BUT KICKS OFF QUICKLY (SHORT-CYCLES, LOW HEAT)

Usually this problem can be traced to airflow problems, especially if the flame is very orangey-colored while it is on (rather than blue.) The solution is to clean out your lint screen or dryer ex-

Figure G-5: Pilot & Unlatch Assembly

Main Gas Valve Solenoid

Latching Cap

Latching Pin

If pilot won't stay lit replace Pilot & Unlatch Diaphragm, Capillary and Sensor (one piece)

Diaphragm

Capillary

Gas Valve

Manual Latching Cap Release

Sensor

Pilot Gas Tube

Pilot Flame

Pilot Orifice

haust. It is an especially common problem in installations where the dryer exhaust runs a long way before venting to the outside. Repair as described in section 2-5.

This may also be caused by a defective flame sensor. Test as described in the section above, "IGNITOR DOESN'T GLOW".

Occasionally this problem can be caused by a bad thermostat. Test as described in section 2-4(c).

PILOT SYSTEM PROBLEMS
PILOT WON'T STAY LIT
(PILOT SYSTEM ONLY)

If the pilot won't stay lit, the pilot & unlatch assembly is usually defective.

The pilot & unlatch assembly (figure G-5) is a safety mechanism. If there is no pilot, it closes off the gas to both the pilot and the main gas valve. This prevents accidental buildup of gas in the dryer cabinet.

The sensor is simply a bulb, like a thermometer bulb, with a liquid inside that expands when the pilot flame heats it. The liquid pushes against a metal diaphragm that holds the spring-loaded gas valve open. If the pilot goes out, the liquid cools and the diaphragm lets the spring close the gas valve.

In order to light the pilot, you must manually hold the valve open for a minute or so, until the sensor heats up enough to hold the valve open.

PILOT BURNS,
BUT FLAME DOES NOT START
(PILOT SYSTEM ONLY)

The gas valve solenoid coil is not opening the main gas valve. Either the gas valve solenoid coil is defective, or the burner is not getting the signal to start burning from the heating control system.

Test the wiring as described previously in the "IGNITOR DOESN'T GLOW" section to see if it is getting the 110-volt signal from the heating control system.

If so, the gas solenoid valve is bad. Replace it.

If the burner isn't getting 110 volts, something is wrong with the heating control system as described previously in the "IGNITOR DOESN'T GLOW" section.

2-4 TESTING ELECTRICAL COMPONENTS

Sometimes you need to read a wiring diagram, to make sure you are not forgetting to check something. Sometimes you just need to find out what color wire to look for to test a component. It is ESPECIALLY important in diagnosing a bad timer.

If you already know how to read a wiring diagram, you can skip this section. If you're one of those folks who's a bit timid around electricity, all I can say is read on, and don't be too nervous. It will come to you. You learned how to use a VOM in Chapter 1, right?

Each component should be labelled clearly on your diagram. Look at figure G-6. The symbols used to represent each component are pretty universal; for example, two different symbols for thermostats are shown, but both have a little square line in them, so you know they're thermostats.

A few notes about reading a wiring diagram:

Notice that in some parts of the diagram, the lines are thicker than in other parts. The wiring and switches that are shown as thick lines are *inside* of the timer.

Also note that since heaters and ignitors are both a type of resistor, they may be shown with the resistor symbol (a zigzag line) or they may have their own square symbol, but they should be clearly marked.

The small circles all over the diagram are terminals. These are places where you can disconnect the wire from the component for testing purposes.

If you see dotted or shaded lines around a group of wires, this is a switch assembly; for example, a temperature or cycle switch assembly. It may also be the timer, but whatever it is, it should be clearly marked on the diagram. Any wiring enclosed by a shaded or dotted box is internal to a switch assembly and must be tested as described in sections 2-4(a) and 2-4(b).

Switches may be numbered or lettered. Those markings can often be found cast or stamped into the switch. To test a switch with a certain marking, mark and disconnect all the wires from your timer. Connect your ohmmeter to the two terminal leads of the switch you want to test. For example, in figure G-6, if you want to test the hi-temp selector switch, connect one lead to the **M** and one to the **H** terminal. Then flick the switch back and forth. It should close and open. If it does, you know that contact inside the switch is good.

Remember that for something to be energized, it must make a complete electrical circuit. You must be able to trace the path that the electricity will take, FROM the wall outlet back TO the wall outlet. This includes not only the component that you suspect, but all switches leading to it.

In Figure G-6(a), which shows a typical *electric* dryer, L1, L2, and N are the main power leads; they go directly to your wall plug. Between L1 and N, you will see 110 volts. Between L2 and N, you will also see 110 volts. But between L1 and L2, you will see 220 volts.

In gas dryers, L1 and L2 will be 110-volt leads. Sometimes they will be labelled L1 and N, but they are still 110 volt leads.

Let's say you need to check out why the heater is not working. Since a burnt out heater element is the most likely cause of this symptom, first test the heater for continuity. If you have good continuity, something else in the circuit that feeds the heater must be defective.

Following the gray-shaded circuit in figure G-6(a), note that the electricity flows from L1 to L2, so this is a 220-volt circuit.

From L1 the electricity flows to the Y-DB switch.

Figure G-6: Typical Wiring Diagram

This switch is located inside of the timer (you know this because it is drawn with thick lines) and it must be closed. The power then goes through the wire to the temperature selector switch. In this example, we have set the temperature on "low." Note that in this machine, on this setting, the electricity flows through both the high-temp and low-temp operating thermostats. Therefore, both thermostats must be closed and show good continuity. The electricity then flows through the high limit thermostat, so it too must be closed and show good continuity.

The electricity flows through the heater, which we have already tested and we know is good. Then the electricity flows through the centrifugal switch, which must be closed, before going back out the main power cord (L2).

To test for the break in the circuit, simply isolate each part of the system (remove the wires from the terminals) and test for continuity. For example, to test the thermostats in our example, pull the wires off each thermostat and test continuity across the thermostat terminals as described in section 2-4(c).

The Y-DB switch is shown in bold lines, so it is inside the timer. For now, let's ignore this switch. (Remember; the timer is the *last* thing you should check; see section 2-4(b).)

That leaves the centrifugal switch, which is only closed when the motor is running. However, if you can identify the proper leads, you can use your alligator jumpers to jump across them. If you do this and the heater kicks on when you turn on the timer, you know the switch is bad.

If NONE of the other components appear to be defective, test the timer as described in section 2-4(b).

To check for a wire break, you would pull each end of a wire off the component and test for continuity through the wire. You may need to use jumpers to extend or even bypass the wire; for example, if one end of the wire is in the control console and the other end in underneath the machine. If there is no continuity, there is a break in the wire! It will then be up to you to figure out exactly where that break is; there is no magic way. If you have a broken wire, look along the length of the wire for pinching or chafing. If there is a place where the wires move, check there first. Even if the insulation is O.K., the wire may be broken inside.

2-4(a) SWITCHES AND SOLENOIDS

Testing switches and solenoids is pretty straightforward. Take all wires off the component and test resistance across it.

Switches should show good continuity when closed and no continuity when open.

Figure G-6(a) Tracing a Wiring Diagram

Solenoids should show SOME resistance, but continuity should be good. If a solenoid shows no continuity, there's a break somewhere in the windings. If it shows no resistance, it's shorted.

2-4(b) TIMERS

The timer is the brain of the dryer. It controls everything in the cycle. In addition to telling the motor when to run, it may also activate the heating circuit or heating control circuits, humidity-sensing circuits, etc.

Figure G-7: Diagnosing Timer Problems

Solid state timers are difficult and expensive to diagnose. If you suspect a timer problem in a solid-state system, you can try replacing it, but remember that it's expensive and non-returnable (being an electrical part.) If you have one of these units that's defective, you can check into the cost of replacing it, but it's been my experience that you usually will end up just replacing the whole dryer or calling a technician. If you do call a technician, make sure you ask up front whether they work on solid-state controls.

Most timers are nothing more than a motor that drives a set of cams which open and close switches. Yet it is one of the most expensive parts in your dryer, so don't be too quick to diagnose it as the problem. Usually the FIRST thing a layman looks at is the timer; it should be the LAST. And don't forget that timers are electrical parts, which are usually non-returnable. If you buy one, and it turns

out *not* to be the problem, you've just wasted the money.

In a wiring diagram, the wiring and switches that are inside the timer will usually be drawn with dark lines.

TIMER DIAGNOSIS

If the timer is not advancing *only in the automatic or humidity control cycle*, (i.e. more dry-less dry on your timer dial) see section 2-4(c) about auto cycles.

If the timer is not advancing in all cycles, well, that's pretty obvious. Replace the timer or timer drive motor, or have it rebuilt as described below.

Timers can be difficult to diagnose. The easiest way is to go through everything else in the malfunctioning system. If none of the other components are bad, then it may be the timer.

Remember that a timer is simply a set of on-off switches. The switches are turned off and on by a cam, which is driven by the timer motor. Timer wires are color-coded or number-coded.

Let's say you've got a motor starting problem. Following the shaded circuit in figure G-7, you test the door switch, push-to-start switch and centrifugal switch. They all test ok. So you think you've traced the problem to your timer.

First unplug the machine. Looking at your wiring diagram, you see that the Y-R switch feeds the drive motor. REMOVE those wires from the timer and touch the test leads to those terminals. Make sure the timer is in the "on" position and slowly turn the timer all the way through a full cycle. (On some timers, you cannot turn the dial while it is on. You must simply test the timer one click at a time. Be patient!)

You should see continuity make and break at least once in the cycle; usually several times. If it doesn't, the internal contacts are bad; replace the timer.

In general, timers cannot be rebuilt by the novice. Check with your parts dealer; if it *can* be rebuilt, he'll get it done for you. If it's a common one, your parts dealer may even have a rebuilt one in stock.

For the most part, if your timer is acting up, you need to replace it. To replace, mark the wires or note the color codes written on the timer. If you need to, you can draw a picture of the terminal arrangement and wire colors. If possible, change over the timer wires one-by-one. It can be easier. If there are any special wiring changes, they will be explained in instructions that come with the new timer.

2-4(c) THERMOSTATS AND OTHER TEMPERATURE CONTROLS

THERMOSTATS (Figure G-8)

A thermostat is basically just a switch that opens or closes according to the temperature that it senses. This switch can be used to turn the heating system (either gas or electric) on and off to maintain a certain air temperature range at a given place in the system.

You can test it as described in section 1-4(b) by testing for continuity across its terminals. A cold *operating* stat or *hi-limit* stat should show continuity. A cold cool-down stat should show no continuity.

Figure G-8: Typical Thermostats

There may be several different thermostats side by side; for example 135 degrees for low temperature, 165 for high temperature, etc. You choose which thermostat is used by selecting the heat setting on the dryer console.

AUTO CYCLES (More Dry-Less Dry)

In an "auto" cycle, the system has some way of sensing how much moisture is in the air inside the dryer drum. If the air is dry, the timer advances more quickly to end the cycle sooner. This is done in one of two ways.

When the air in the drum is moist, the water in it absorbs heat to evaporate. This keeps the air temperature lower, and it takes longer to heat up. The thermostat on the drum exhaust will keep the heating system on longer. In these systems, that same thermostat controls the timer motor; while the heating system is on, the timer motor is not running, and vice-versa. As the clothes get drier, the exhaust air temperature increases more quickly and stays hotter, so the heating system doesn't stay on for as long, and the timer motor runs more, and the cycle ends sooner.

The thermostats in these machines have three leads. One side goes to the timer motor, the other to the heating system. These thermostats are also difficult to test without any way to heat them up. But they're pretty cheap. If the symptoms lead you to suspect that yours is defective, just replace it.

Besides heating more slowly, moist air also conducts electricity better than dry air. So another way the engineers design a humidity sensor is to put two electrical contacts inside the dryer drum. The electrical currents conducted by the air are so low that an electronic circuit is needed to sense when the air is moist, but essentially the same thing happens in this system as in the other. When the air is moist, the timer motor doesn't run as often. When the air is dry, the timer motor runs longer and times out sooner.

The sensors in these machines tend to get coated with gummy stuff, especially if you use a lot of fabric softener in the wash or starch in ironing. If the timer is not advancing during the auto cycle, this is likely what has happened. Try scrubbing the sensors with a little 409 to get it off. In extreme cases, use a little rubbing alcohol as a solvent. The circuit board could have gone bad, too; there is no good way to test it without a lot of expensive equipment. If you think it has gone bad, it probably has. Replace it.

SPECIAL NOTE: *In electric dryers with an automatic cycle, a special problem exists. The problem is that the heater operates on 220 volts, but the timer motor runs on 110 volts. There is a resistor in the system to cut down the voltage (see figure G-7 and if this resistor is bad, you will see the same symptoms as if the thermostat was bad: the timer motor will not run in the automatic cycle. If you have one of these dryers, make sure you test the resistor for continuity, in addition to the thermostat.*

If a thermostat fails into a closed position, there is a danger that the heating system will continue operating until something catches fire. To prevent this, there is a high-temperature thermostat that will cut out the entire heating system.

There is no way to repair thermostats. Replace any that are bad.

OTHER TEMPERATURE CONTROLS

Selecting which thermostat is used may be done inside the timer, or there may be a separate multi-switch that accomplishes this. Test internal timer switches as described in section 2-4(b).

Separate temperature selector switches are tested either by measuring continuity through each contact (figure G-9) or by jumping across the two correct terminals with your alligator jumpers.

2-4(d) DRIVE MOTORS AND CENTRIFUGAL START SWITCH

A motor that is trying to start, but can't for whatever reason, is using one heckuva lot of electricity. So much, in fact, that if it is allowed to continue being energized in a stalled state, it will start burning wires. To prevent this, an overload switch is installed on motors to cut power to them if they don't start within a certain amount of time.

If the motor is trying to start, but can't, you will hear certain things. First will be a click, followed immediately by a buzzing sound. Then, after about 5 to 20 seconds of buzzing, another click and the buzzing will stop. The sounds will keep repeating every minute or two. In some extreme cases, you may even smell burning.

If you hear the motor doing this, but it won't start, disconnect power and take all the load off it. For example, disconnect the drive belt, and make sure nothing is jamming the blower wheel. The motor should turn easily by hand.

Try to start the motor again. If it still won't start, the motor is bad. If you have an ammeter, the stalled motor will be drawing 10 to 20 amps or more.

STARTING SWITCH

Dryers have a centrifugal starting switch mounted piggyback on the motor. There are many sets of contacts inside the switch, and each design is different, even among dryers of the same brand. Testing the switch is most easily accomplished by replacing it.

Remember that starting switches are electrical parts, which are generally not returnable. If you test the switch by replacing it, and the problem turns out to be the motor itself, you will probably not be able to return the starting switch for a refund. But they're pretty cheap, and if it *is* the problem, you just saved yourself the best part of a hundred bucks for a new motor.

If the motor is stalled (buzzing and/or tripping out on the overload switch) and the starting switch tests O.K., the motor is bad. Replace it.

NOTE: Many motors have the belt pulley pressed onto the motor shaft. However, a replacement motor may come without a pulley. When buying a new motor, make sure that the pulley can be changed over, or else get a new pulley with the new motor. It may save you a second trip to the parts dealer.

Figure G-9: Testing a Typical Selector Switch

TEMPERATURE SELECTOR SWITCH

Low Temp Setting:
Good Continuity from M to L
No Continuity from M to H

High Temp Setting:
Good Continuity from M to H
No Continuity from M to L

2-4(e) IGNITORS

You can test the ignitor by testing for resistance across the element. (See figure G-10) A good ignitor will show quite a bit of resistance, between about 50 and 600 ohms. A bad ignitor will usually show no continuity at all.

2-4(f) ELECTRIC HEATERS

Electric heater elements are tested by measuring continuity across them. Like ignitors, they should show quite a bit of resistance, and defective heaters will usually show no continuity at all.

If none of the above works, the internal ducting or blower fan is clogged or malfunctioning. To open the dryer and clean out the ducting, see chapter 3 or 4 about your model.

NOTE: Late model machines CAN be operated with the front of the cabinet taken off, but since there is nothing enclosing the dryer drum, there will be no airflow, and the heating system will not operate properly. In fact, doing this will overheat the heating system.

2-5 DRIVE BELTS AND TENSIONERS

To access the drive belt(s), see chapter 3 or 4 about your model.

If you see any of the problems pictured in figure G-11, replace the belt.

It is important for the belt tensioner to be operating properly. Check for broken springs. Also check that the tensioner idler roller spins freely.

Figure G-10: Testing Ignitors

Remove leads from ignitor and touch VOM test leads to terminals

Figure G-11: Typical Belt Problems

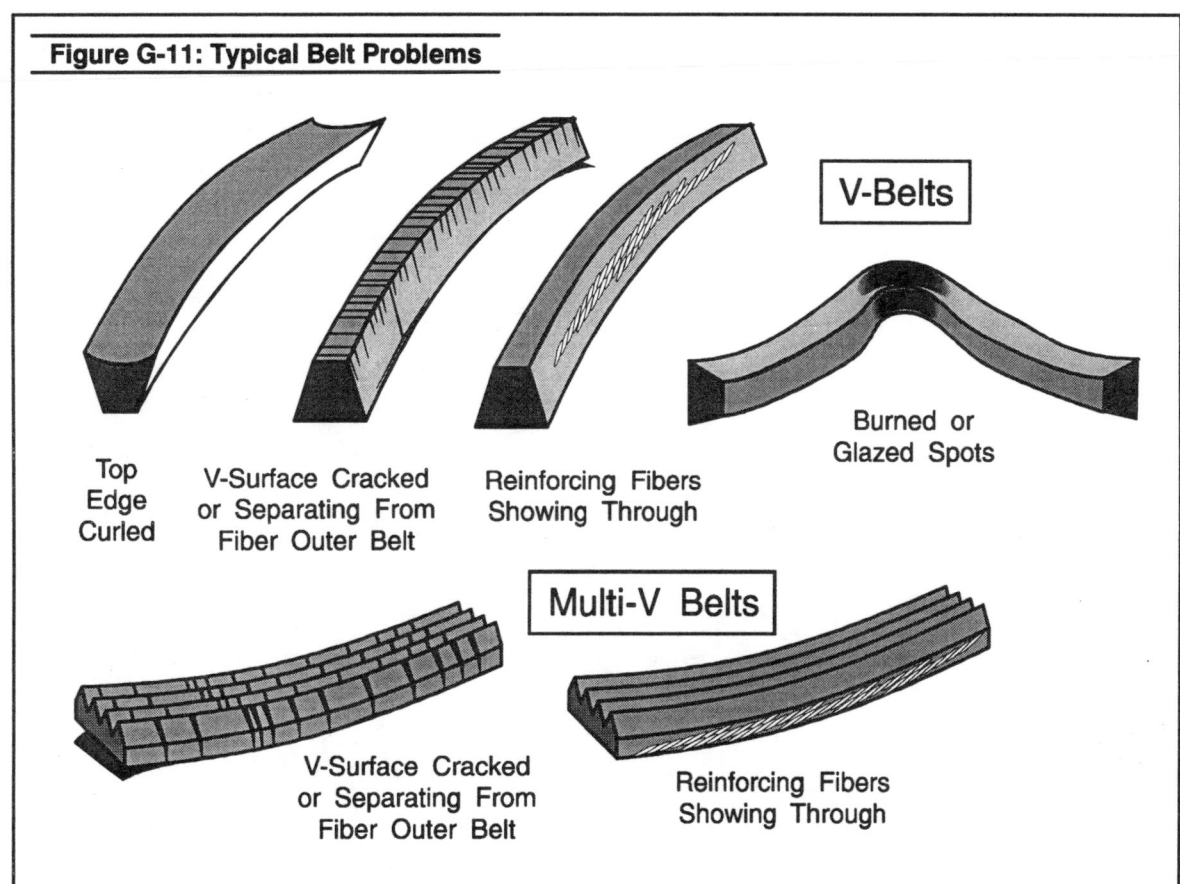

Top Edge Curled

V-Surface Cracked or Separating From Fiber Outer Belt

Reinforcing Fibers Showing Through

V-Belts

Burned or Glazed Spots

Multi-V Belts

V-Surface Cracked or Separating From Fiber Outer Belt

Reinforcing Fibers Showing Through

Chapter 3

LATE MODEL MACHINES

In the mid-1980's, Maytag began selling a completely redesigned dryer. Prior to that, they sold a design called a "halo of heat" model. (See Chapter 4)

The easiest way to tell them apart is that in the "halo" models, the lint screen is inside the center rear of the drum, whereas the late model Maytag machines have the lint screen in the front of the cabinet, at the bottom of the door opening.

Figure ML-1 shows the general layout of these machines.

The drum is supported at the front by two small glides beneath the drum. The rear of the drum is supported by rollers.

The cabinet is solid on three sides, so almost everything is accessed through the front of the machine. There is a small inspection panel on the bottom right, as you look at the back of the machine, through which you can get to the belt tensioner and idler pulley.

The blower fan is mounted directly to the front of the drive motor. The drive pulley and belt come off the rear of the motor, and the belt goes completely around the drum. The motor and blower are on the left side of the baseplate of the machine. A spring-loaded idler, mounted to the motor baseplate, keeps tension on the belt.

In gas models the burner is on the right side of the baseplate of the machine. It is accessible through the small inspection door on the lower right front of the machine. In electric models, the heater is located in a cylindrical heater box in the same place as the burner chamber.

Figure ML-1: General Layout

Drum Rollers (Rear Supports)

Drive Belt

Drive Motor

Blower

Lint Screen

Gas Burner Chamber or Electric Heater Element Box

Airflow

Drum Glides (Drum Front Supports)

Heat Riser

Operating thermostats in these machines are located on the front of the blower exhaust housing. Hi-limit stats are located on top of the burner chamber in gas models, and directly on top of the heater box in electric models.

3-2 COMMON PROBLEMS

The most common problems in these machines are as follows:

1) Loud rumbling or banging noise, getting progressively worse over time, or squeaky sounds coming from the drum support rollers. Replace as described in section 3-4.

2) Heating problems as described in chapter 2.

3) Drum doesn't turn, caused by a broken belt. Replace as described in section 3-4.

4) No airflow. These machines seem to be particularly susceptible to getting clogged up with lint. Remove the front panel and clean out the blower as described in section 3-3.

5) These machines seem to be susceptible to things slipping past the lint screen, especially pens and pencils and such. If this happens, you will hear a loud grinding sound that seems like it resounds through the whole machine. Open the blower cover and inspect the blower wheel as described in section 3-3. Replace the blower wheel if the blades are chewed up.

Figure ML-2: Opening the Cabinet

Remove two screws, lift cabinet front and disengage top clips

Remove two screws inside cabinet and lift cabinet top

3-3 OPENING THE CABINET (Figure ML-2)

Remove the two screws at the bottom of the cabinet front. Lift the bottom of the front panel until the clips at the top of the panel disengage from the top. Be careful to note the position of any door switch or other wiring and disconnect it as you remove the panel.

***NOTE:** Late model machines CAN be operated with the front of the cabinet taken off, but since there is nothing enclosing the dryer drum, there will be no airflow, and the heating system will not operate properly. In fact, doing this will overheat the heating system.*

To lift the cabinet top, remove the two screws beneath the front corners.

BLOWER

To inspect, clean or replace the blower wheel, remove the blower inlet cover. The blower wheel is held onto the motor shaft with a spring clip.

3-4 DRUM REMOVAL

To inspect and/or replace drum glides, belts or electric heater elements, you must remove the drum as follows:

1) Open the inspection panel on the back of the machine and release belt tension.

2) Remove the cabinet front as described in section 3-3.

3) Remove the four screws from the front bulkhead as shown in figure ML-3. While holding the drum in place, lift out the bulkhead and set it aside. You can now lift out the drum.

Figure ML-3: Front Bulkhead

Front Bulkhead

Remove four bulkhead mounting screws

Blower Inlet Cover

The drum glides are on the lower front corners of the inside of the bulkhead. They are riveted in place. If you need to change them, you must drill out the rivets and rivet new ones in place. The rivets come with the glide kit.

The drum support roller shafts are held onto the rear bulkhead with a nut. (Figure ML-4) Remove the nut to remove the roller wheels.

The front and rear drum seals can also be inspected for wear at this point. They are glued onto the front and back bulkheads. If you need to replace them, you must scrape off the old adhesive and glue in new ones.

In electric models, the heater element is located inside the heater box on the right side of the baseplate of the machine. Test it for continuity as described in Chapter 2, and if defective, replace the heater box.

Don't forget to check that the belt tension idler spins smoothly. Replace if sticking or binding, by pulling off the spring clip that holds the idler pulley to its shaft.

BELT REPLACEMENT

Getting the belt around the idler in these machines can be a real son-of-a-gun. For one thing, the belt is sort of upside-down compared to other machines; the flat side goes against the drum and idler. (See figure ML-5) There's also a lot of spring tension.

Try to position the belt as closely as possible on the old skid marks on the drum. And after you get it on, slowly rotate the drum a few times to make sure the belt doesn't jump off the idler.

Figure ML-4: Rear Bulkhead and Drum Rollers

Rear Bulkhead

Drum Rollers are held to rear bulkhead by nut on back side of bulkhead.

Figure ML-5: Drive Belt Tensioner

Note: Flat side of belt goes against drum and idler pulley.

Toothed side of belt goes against motor pinion.

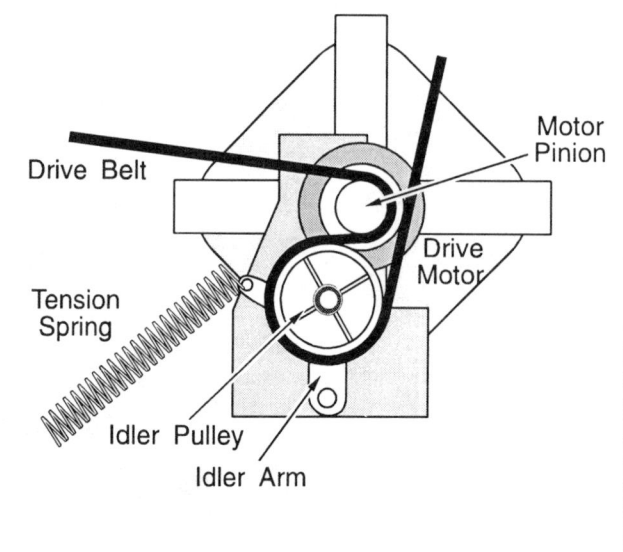

Drive Belt

Tension Spring

Idler Pulley

Idler Arm

Motor Pinion

Drive Motor

Chapter 4

EARLY-MODEL MACHINES
("Halo of Heat" Models)

4-1 MACHINE LAYOUT

The "halo of heat" name comes from the fact that in electric models, there is a single circular heater element around the front of the drum. The "halo" actually encircles the front door opening.

There are no front drum supports in these machines; the drum is completely supported by the shaft at the rear of the drum. The blower housing in these machines is a structural member and it contains the bearings that support the drum shaft. A frame (called a "spider") holds up the blower housing. (Figure MH-1) The blower wheel itself is concentric with the drum and runs on the drum shaft.

There are two belts at the rear of these machines. One comes off the drive motor and drives the blower and a tensioner/idler. The second runs from the tensioner/idler and drives the drum.

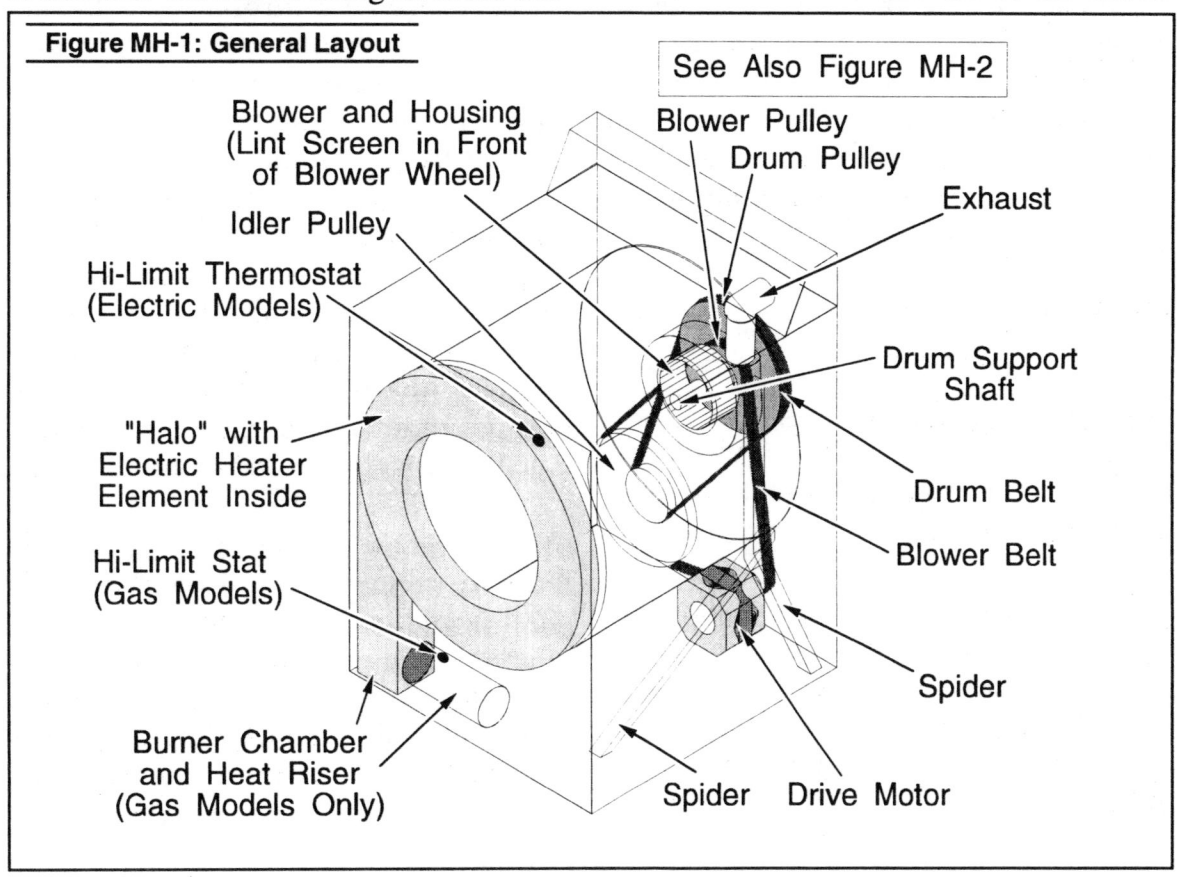

Figure MH-1: General Layout

See Also Figure MH-2

Blower and Housing (Lint Screen in Front of Blower Wheel)
Idler Pulley
Hi-Limit Thermostat (Electric Models)
"Halo" with Electric Heater Element Inside
Hi-Limit Stat (Gas Models)
Burner Chamber and Heat Riser (Gas Models Only)
Blower Pulley
Drum Pulley
Exhaust
Drum Support Shaft
Drum Belt
Blower Belt
Spider
Spider   Drive Motor

All gas models have pilot ignition. None have electric or glo-type ignitors. The gas burner and burner chamber on these machines runs across the bottom front of the baseplate, with the gas valve on the right and the heat riser duct on the left. Access to the valve is through a burner inspection cover on the lower right front of the machine.

The heating control system is slightly different in these machines, especially in electronic control models. They are set up to sense the moisture in the clothes using humidity sensors in the baffles (vanes) inside the drum. Once the proper humidity is reached inside the drum, the heating system shuts down, but the cool-down thermostat keeps the motor running until the clothes cool off a bit. Failure of this system can cause a few odd symptoms as described in section 4-2.

The operating thermostats in these machines are located on top of the blower housing, inside the back of the machine. If there are two thermostats in that location, the one on the right is a cool-down thermostat and should be *open* when cold. The hi-limit thermostat is located at the top of the halo on electric models, and on top of the burner chamber on gas models.

4-2 COMMON PROBLEMS

The most common problems with these machines are:

1) The belts wear out or break. The symptom is that the drum does not turn. If you replace one belt, you must replace them both or the machine will not run right. See section 4-3 to replace.

2) In gas models, there is a problem when the cabinet feels uncomfortably hot to the touch. The front felt seals deteriorate or burn, and hot air escapes straight from the halo into the cabinet. To replace them, you must remove the whole cabinet from the machine as described in section 4-4.

3) The bearing on the blower wheel seizes, and the blower wheel locks up. The symptom is that the exhaust will be weak or non-existent, and usually the dryer drum won't turn. Replace the blower wheel as described in section 4-3.

4) Heating problems. Diagnose and repair as described in Chapter 2. Electric heater elements can be tested by removing the cabinet as described in section 4-4.

5) In electronic control models, the motor sometimes will not shut off. The heat also keeps cycling on and off long past when the clothes are dry. This is usually caused by the humidity sensors within the drum being gummed up with starch or other deposits. The sensors look like copper wires or silver bars imbedded into the baffles (vanes) of the dryer drum. If your dryer won't shut off, try cleaning the baffles. You may have to scrape a little, but be careful not to damage the sensors imbedded into the vane.

6) If the motor doesn't shut off, but the heat *has* stopped cycling on and off, the cool-down thermostat may be stuck in a closed position. (The cool-down is the thermostat on the right, as you look into the back of the dryer.) The heating system shuts down when the humidity sen-

sors sense that the clothes are dry, and these thermostats keep the motor running for a short time after that to cool down the clothes. Unlike other thermostats, these cool-down thermostats should be *open* when the dryer is cool. If they are *closed* when cool, the contacts inside are welded shut and the motor won't stop running. Test the thermostat and replace if you suspect it's defective.

The same symptom may be caused by the machine not being grounded. These machines MUST be grounded, either through the third prong of the wall plug or directly from the cabinet to a house ground. If you have recently moved the machine, and now it won't shut off, check to make sure the machine is grounded somehow.

7) In very early machines, the motor pulley was made of a pot metal material. Strange symptom, but the *belt* can actually wear out the *pulley*. If this happens, the proper belt tension cannot be maintained and the dryer drum will turn very weakly. These pot metal pullies are easily recognized, as they had a greenish color. Replace it with a steel pulley, available at your parts dealer.

4-3 REAR ACCESS, BELT REPLACEMENT, BLOWER SERVICE

To change the belts or blower wheel, open the rear panel by removing the screws that hold it on.

The idler pulley on the lower right, as you look in the back of the dryer, (figure MH-2) is spring loaded and keeps tension on the belts. Remove the tension spring to remove the belts.

Once the belts are removed, check that both the idler and drum pullies are turning freely, without binding.

To get to the blower wheel, remove the drum pulley. The small pulley beneath is the blower pulley, which is one piece with the blower wheel. Try turning this pulley by hand around the drum shaft. If it is binding, replace the blower wheel.

To remove the blower wheel, First remove the exhaust elbow. Then remove the blower housing cover screws and the cover will come off the housing.

Figure MH-2: Rear of Machine, Cabinet Removed

Blower Pulley (beneath drum pulley)
Blower Housing
Operating Thermostat
Cool-Down Thermostat
Drum Pulley
Blower Belt
Spider
Drum Belt
Drive Motor
Idler Pulley
Belt Tension Spring

4-4 ACCESS TO THE HALO AREA

To test or replace the electric heating elements, door switch, or felt seal, you must remove the entire cabinet.

Unplug the dryer and remove the back as described in section 4-3.

Disconnect the motor wiring harness plug at the motor. Remove the harness from any routing clips holding it to the spider. Also disconnect the wire leads to the operating thermostats.

Remove the two cabinet mounting screws at the bottom rear corners of the dryer. Also remove the three screws at the bottom of each side of the cabinet; these hold the cabinet to the baseplate.

In gas models, the halo is connected to the baseplate of the dryer and stays with it when you remove the cabinet. In electric models, the halo comes off with the cabinet. Therefore, in gas models, you must also remove the four screws from inside the dryer door (Figure MH-3) that connect the halo to the cabinet front.

Figure MH-3: Halo Mounting Screws

To remove cabinet:

Remove four halo mounting screws inside dryer door (gas models only)

Also remove cabinet-to-baseplate mounting screws

You can now lift the cabinet off. Be careful, it is heavy. Also take care that the wiring harnesses don't get tangled up in anything as the cabinet comes off.

In gas models, there is a felt seal between the halo and the drum. (Figure MH-4) The seal has two pieces; the seal itself, and a felt band which keeps the seal in tension around the drum. Inspect it for burning or damage. A seal kit is available from your parts dealer. To replace, remove the halo.

In electric models, inspect the heater element and test it for continuity. Replace if defective. Also check the insulators that hold the element in place for cracking and replace if defective.

Figure MH-4: Front Seal

Felt Seal and Band

Drum

Halo

Index

Also Available from EB Publishing

Brand-Specific Dryer & Top-Loading Washer Manuals!

for those who want a little LESS...
Our brand-specific manuals have the same high quality instructions and illustrations
as our all-brand manuals, at a new low price!

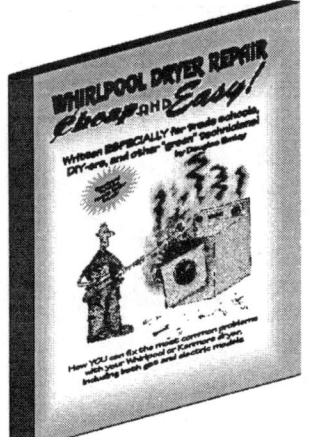

2000 Edition
Whirlpool Dryer Repair
ISBN 1-890386-42-1   Part No. EBWD

2000 Edition
Whirlpool Washer Repair
ISBN 1-890386-41-3   Part No. EBWW

Whirlpool-brand manuals include
Kenmore, Kitchenaid, Estate
and Roper Brand Machines

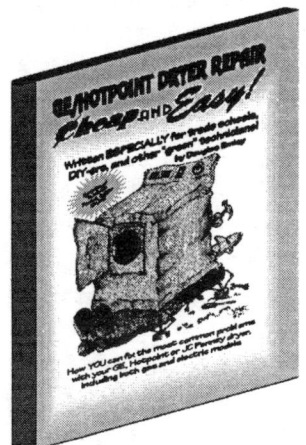

2000 Edition
GE/Hotpoint Dryer Repair
ISBN 1-890386-44-8   Part No. EBGD

2000 Edition
GE/Hotpoint Washer Repair
ISBN 1-890386-43-X   Part No. EBGW

GE-brand manuals include
Hotpoint, late-model RCA, and
JC Penney (Penncrest) Brand Machines

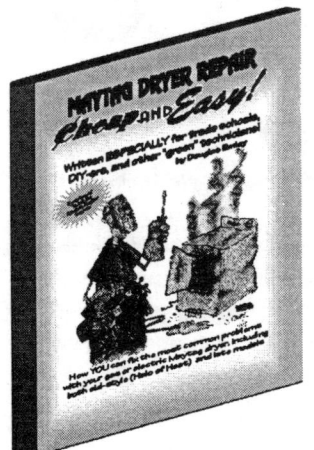

2000 Edition
Maytag Dryer Repair
ISBN 1-890386-46-4   Part No. EBMD

2000 Edition
Maytag Washer Repair
ISBN 1-890386-45-6   Part No. EBMW

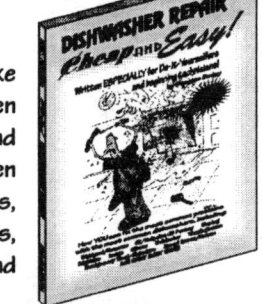